Peril In Evans Woods

Peril In

Louise Mandrell and Ace Collins

Children's Holiday Adventure Series

Volume 6

THE SUMMIT GROUP

1227 West Magnolia, Suite 500, Fort Worth, Texas 76104

© 1993 by Louise Mandrell and Ace Collins. All rights reserved.

93   10   9   8   7   6   5   4   3   2   1

Jacket and Book Design by Cheryl Corbitt

PUBLISHER'S CATALOGING-IN-PUBLICATION DATA (Prepared by Quality Books Inc.)
Mandrell, Louise.
    Peril In Evans Woods / Louise Mandrell and Ace Collins; illustrated by Paige Frailey.
    p. cm. – (Holiday adventure series; v. 6)
    Summary: In seventeenth century New Hampshire, Aaron McGregor must go into the
haunted Evans Woods in the middle of a nighttime thunderstorm to save his sister's life. Set on
Good Friday, the story gives a taste of life during the early days of America.
    ISBN 1-56530-035-1; $12.95
    1. Good Friday – Fiction. 2. Easter – Fiction. 3. Frontier and pioneer life – New Hampshire –
Fiction. 4. New Hampshire – Fiction. I. Collins, Ace. II. Frailey, Paige, ill. III. Title. IV. Series:
Mandrell, Louise. Holiday adventure series; v. 6.
PZ7. M31254Pe 1993
[Fic]
QB193-20130

Evans Woods

Illustrated by Paige Frailey

THE SUMMIT GROUP

Nine-year-old Aaron McGregor hated the long walk from school to his New Hampshire home. He didn't mind walking the three miles over rocky paths. But he dreaded having to venture so close to Evans Woods. Like all the school children and most of the adults in and around his New Hampshire home, Aaron was afraid of what lurked in the deep, dark shadows just beyond the creek. After all, the Mayflower had landed only sixty years ago, and Plymouth was still a young town. There was much that was strange and different about this new land.

Some people scoffed at the stories and said there was nothing to be afraid of. But others swore that evil spirits ruled the woods and that strange things happened to anyone who went there.

His own father had been one of those who discounted such tales. But one day, after he had gone hunting in the woods, he caught a terrible chill. He was sick for days. And even though the doctor had told his mother that Henry McGregor had died of pneumonia, others claimed it was a curse that took the life of the strong farmer.

Aaron's father had always been a religious man. He had often told Aaron that all such superstitions were nonsense and that evil spirits didn't haunt Evans Woods. Yet others, even some elders from their church, insisted that any person who walked into that forbidding forest, even in the daylight, was doomed to die. They whispered darkly of terrible deaths and unexplained disappearances.

But the woods were on Aaron's way home from school, and he had no choice but to pass them each day.

They were but a quarter of a mile from the McGregor farm. Yet, when near the woods, he ran at full speed and made sure that he passed that way only in the daylight. Even then he swore that he could feel someone looking at him.

If Aaron had taken the time to search beyond the mysterious blackness he would have noticed that spring had arrived. Flowers were blooming, birds had returned to the trees, and the air was beginning to exhibit a bit of warmth. The last patches of winter snow could be seen only in the deep shadow, and colors of all kinds and hues abounded in the meadows. Yet, the young boy, clad in the black and white clothing worn by all members of his faith, was running too hard and was far too afraid to take note of anything but those dark, evil woods.

Aaron could breathe easier when the forest was behind him; and, as he neared his family's farm, he saw his mother coming from the barn. Following her was Aaron's three-year-old sister, Mary, her violet eyes filled with mischief.

Nodding her head in a greeting, Elizabeth McGregor, barely thirty but already bent from the long years of hard farm work, held up her hand. "Why art thou running?" she inquired in her proper manner.

"The woods!" her son exclaimed, pointing behind him.

"Aaron McGregor," she scolded, "how often have I told thee that there is nothing in the woods that is not here around the farm? Your father, God rest his soul, knew it and on many occasions he told thee that there was nothing there to trouble thee."

"Yes, Mother," Aaron answered.

Shaking her head, Elizabeth added, "Now time is wasting, and thou must have thy chores finished before the sun goes down. So hurry thee on with thy work!"

An hour later, Aaron had finished stacking the wood his mother had chopped earlier. After that he gathered the eggs and milked the cow. As he entered their small, wooden home, he was not surprised to see his mother sitting at the table reading the family Bible.

"It is good that thou hast finished," she said, looking up. "It will be dark in just a few minutes, and I feel a storm coming."

Setting the eggs and milk on the table, Aaron walked across the room to the fireplace. The evening meal was steaming in a large pot resting on the hearth.

"What is for supper, Mother?" he asked.

"I used some berries and vegetables to make a stew," she replied.

"Is there no meat?" Aaron questioned.

"What is left is rotten," she answered. "We will have no more meat for some time."

Aaron sighed sadly. "Why did we ever leave Scotland?" he asked. "If we were still there, we would be having mutton and bread."

Looking up from the Bible, his mother frowned, "Bite thy tongue. It was an act of bravery that brought us here. Others wanted to come. They wanted to come to a land where people can believe as they wish, say what they want. But they heard the stories about warlike savages and an ocean filled with demons and monsters, and they stayed behind. Your father was a man of faith and courage. He knew that there would be hardships, but he also knew that it would be worth the price of facing his fears. Your father brought us here so that we could be free to worship God in our own way," she said proudly. Then, softening her tone, she asked, "Dost thou remember what he did when we boarded the boat to leave for the colonies?"

"Yes," Aaron answered. "He read the first verse in the Bible and said, 'Thank God, we are finally free.' But Mother, we were not in prison in Scotland, and there life was not so hard. If we had stayed, Father might still be alive."

Shaking her head, his mother whispered, "Thou art too young to understand that many things can place thee in chains. Now, let us eat our supper."

Aaron's mother set the table while Aaron washed his hands in a small basin. As he dried them on an old cloth, he glanced about the room.

"Where is Mary?" he asked.

Turning from the fire, his mother pointed to the corner, but the girl was not there. Quickly walking to the cabin's other room, she peered into the shadows. Dashing to the door, she hurriedly stepped out into the dark night. She ran to the barn, but found nothing. She called her daughter's name again and again, but the child didn't answer.

"Aaron," she cried out, "she is gone!"

"The woods!" he cried.

"What?" his mother asked, in a panic.

"She has gone to the woods!" Aaron insisted.

"How dost thou know?" the woman inquired frantically.

"She saw a rabbit go in there yesterday," he responded, "and I kept her from following. She wanted to catch it for a pet. She must have gone to look for it."

As the two of them stared out into the darkness, a streak of lightning lit up the night skies. It was followed by a loud crash of thunder. The wind picked up, and a hint of moisture could be felt in the breeze.

"We must get help," his mother said.

Shaking his head, Aaron responded, "There is no time. We must find her now."

Then, without thinking, he said, "Mother, thou must stay here at home in case Mary returns. I will go and look for her."

And before his mother could stop him, Aaron dashed off toward Evans Woods. He ran hard and fast, stopping only when he reached the edge of the eerie stand of trees. Suddenly he didn't feel as brave. His heart was pounding: and a bright flash of lightning, followed by the roll of thunder, made him start to tremble.

Aaron stared into the forest, and he was sure he caught glimpses of goblins darting from trunk to trunk. They were waiting for him; he was certain of it. He backed away from the woods, muttering "Mary is probably in the meadow. I will look for her there. She *couldn't* be in the woods." But just as he was about to run through the field toward the meadow, he heard a soft cry from within the trees and shadows.

Turning quickly, he yelled, "Mary!" Then he waited for her reply.

Again the lightning flashed, and this time it struck a tree just a few hundred yards from where he stood. The old oak blew apart in a mighty explosion, and Aaron fell to the ground, terrified. He got up only when he heard a voice faintly cry out, "Aaron?"

Still shaking, he studied the woods. The voice had to be his sister's, but what if it were the voice of an evil spirit trying to trick him? How could he be sure? As he hesitated, his father's words came back to him.

"Aaron, there is nothing to fear in the woods that is not in the meadow. If thou shouldst find thyself frightened, here in this land thou canst freely call upon the Lord to help thee. It is thy right."

Aaron had never really understood what his father's words meant, but he knew that he had to enter Evans Woods. So he prayed for protection, and for the courage to face his fears. He asked God to bring Mary safely home. Taking a deep breath, he slowly stepped into the woods, past the first stand of trees and onto a rocky path.
He stood still until another flash of lightning assured him that nothing was in his way. Then he ran forward a few more steps.

"Mary!" he called out when he stopped. "Mary?"

But she didn't answer. The farther he walked and the deeper into the woods he searched, the denser the forest became. Soon, the flashes of lightning did little to show him the path. But, with hands outstretched, he continued. Then, from out of nowhere, something or someone clasped a spindly arm around his throat.

Fear surged through his body, and Aaron tried to jump forward, only to have the arm pull more tightly around his neck. He said a quick prayer as he reached up to grab his attacker. The arm was thin, stiff, and slimy; and, judging from the way it reached down to lift his chin, it belonged to someone very tall.

"What dost thou want with me?" Aaron whispered. "What good is a lad to a spirit?"

His attacker did not respond. Aaron's heart was beating so hard he thought it would burst through his chest. He tried to run, but the arm held fast, pulling him back. Then, from somewhere to his left, he heard a soft whisper.

"Mary!" he cried out.

"Aaron?" came the muffled reply.

The spirits must have her too, he thought. He *had* to get Mary away from them. He thought of his father, facing the mighty ocean in a small ship, and he readied himself to confront his enemy. He waited for the next burst of bright lightning; and, when it flashed, he grabbed the being's arm with both of his hands and whipped around. What he saw took him completely by surprise.

"A vine!" he gulped. "I was being held prisoner by a vine!" Just as Aaron stepped out from under it, a cold downpour let loose from the heavens. Now Mary would be soaked, and she might catch a chill if he didn't find her soon. Aaron called again, "Mary, art thou there?"

Between deafening crashes of thunder, he heard a small cry. Scrambling up a rock in the direction of the sound, he tripped over a fallen tree and began to roll down a mossy hill. Crashing through the bushes and over rocks, he finally landed, scraped and bruised, in a mud-filled bog. He sat still for a moment, recovering his breath and hoping to hear his sister's voice. But he heard something much different.

From the top of a ridge came a long, low growl.
It sounded more wicked than anything Aaron had ever
heard. A monster! Struggling to stand, he discovered that
the mud and mire held him in place as though they were
glue. The more he fought, the deeper he sank. The bright
lightning flashed and a loud crash echoed, and Aaron
frantically searched the darkness for something he could
use to pull himself from his muddy trap.

The howling continued, and it seemed to be getting
nearer. Each time Aaron heard it, it seemed a few feet
closer. He felt certain it was coming to get him.

"Aaron," a child's voice cried out.

"Mary?" Aaron called back.

"Aaron," she said again.

Peering through the night, Aaron saw his sister
running down the hill toward him, sobbing.

"Wait," he cried. "Do not come near me. I am stuck
and thou wilt be too if thee falls in this bog. Wait there."

With all his might, Aaron worked his legs forward one
at a time. Inch by inch, reassuring the sobbing toddler the
whole while, he came closer to the bank. When he was
just a few feet from freedom, a flash of lightning bright-
ened the woods, and Aaron saw, in that second, a huge
wolf up on the hilltop. Its yellow eyes glowed, and its
mouth hung open wide.

Now that it had been spotted, the animal made its
move. Charging down the hill, it bounded across the
rocks toward the bog. Aaron knew the wolf would avoid
the sticky mud. It was Mary the animal was after.

"Run, Mary, run!" Aaron shrieked as the wolf
bounded closer.

The little girl just stared, frozen with terror.

Frantically pushing through the muck, Aaron grabbed for the rocks along the shore, but they were wet from the rain, and he couldn't hang on.

The wolf, now within a few feet, raced toward Mary at full speed. In a panic, Aaron lunged out and tried to hit the creature's head. He missed, but as the gray mass of fur streaked by, Aaron's fingers closed around the wolf's massive tail. Clamping down tightly, Aaron hung on and

was jerked with such force that he was pulled free of the bog. When he hit the ground, he lost his grip. Meanwhile, the wolf, yelping in pain, forgot Mary and whirled to face its attacker.

Jumping to his feet, Aaron stood as tall as he was able to stand and stared straight into the wolf's flashing eyes. The beast seemed confused by this show of fearlessness. Suddenly it turned and ran back up the hill.

Overwhelmed with relief, Aaron raced over to Mary, scooped her up in his arms, and ran back through the woods toward home.

As the two emerged from the trees the rain let up. Secure in the knowledge that nothing would now hurt them, Aaron sat Mary on the ground and sighed, "We are free." Then, taking her hand, he lifted her to her feet and they walked across the meadow. Their mother was waiting for them at the end of the path.

"Thank God," she cried as Aaron handed his sister to her.

"She is all right," he said, trying not to cry himself. He was so thankful to be home, and to have his sister safe, that he could barely speak.

An hour later, after Mary had fallen asleep and Aaron had washed and eaten his stew, Aaron and his mother sat down at the table.

"Thou wert a brave lad," his mother said when she had heard the events of the night. Then she smiled. "I know of few men in the village who have successfully fought a vine and a wolf in the same night."

Aaron nodded shyly, but then grew serious. "I have never felt so helpless as I did in the bog," he said. "The wolf was going for Mary, and I could do nothing. Then, when I was pulled free, I felt as if nothing could stop me."

"Aaron," his mother asked as she opened the Bible, "dost thou know what day this is?"

"Friday."

"Not just any Friday," she explained. "It is Good Friday, the day Christ was nailed to the cross. In His time, people couldn't worship in the manner they chose. If they did, they sometimes paid with their lives. In much of the world it is still that way. But here we are free to choose.

"Thou knowest the man who runs the market in town?" she continued.

"Mr. Solash?" Aaron responded.

"He is of a different religion than we are," she told the boy. "In his own country, he was often beaten and even cast in jail for what he believed. Yet, here he can worship in the manner he chooses. For the first time, he is free."

Reaching across the table, Aaron's mother picked up one of the eggs Aaron had gathered earlier in the day. Holding it up to the light, she studied it for a few moments, then handed it to her son.

"This egg," she said, "represents a new beginning. Christians have long claimed the egg as the perfect symbol for this season. Beneath this fragile shell is a promise of new life. Yet, even with that promise, sometimes a chick must fight hard to free itself from the shell, and even then its life can be difficult.

"Your father fought hard to leave a place where he felt as trapped as thou didst in that bog. He saw others taking away his family's chances for a free life, a free choice. He gave up his friends and an easier life in order to choose his own religion. So did Mr. Solash, and thousands of others. That is the reason many people have come to this land. On this Easter, we celebrate not only because we believe that God gave us a second chance to begin again, but that He gave us this place where we could build a country for all who want and need freedom."

"That is what Father meant!" Aaron exclaimed. "That is why he read the first verse in the Bible. This is a place for new beginnings."

Smiling, his mother added, "Today thou wentedst into the woods, saved thy sister, faced the evil spirits of superstition, and returned a man. Thy father's sacrifice in coming here is bearing fruit in his son. Thou art growing up free!"

Easter is a time for marking the
Christian holiday of the resurrection of Christ.
It is celebrated on the first Sunday
after the first full moon after the Spring equinox.
The equinox is the time when night and day
are of equal lengths at the equator.
Hence, from year to year Easter can fall on any
Sunday between March 22 and April 25.
It was first widely recognized in the
U.S. during the height of the Civil War.
Mourning families used this time
of faith to renew their own belief in the
eternal lives of those who had died in battle.
One of the most cherished
symbols of this holiday is the Easter egg.
The Easter egg traditionally
symbolizes new life.

BOOKS IN THE HOLIDAY ADVENTURE SERIES

New Year's Day • *Martin Luther King Day* • *Valentine's Day*
Presidents' Day • *St. Patrick's Day* • *Easter* • *Mother's Day* • *Memorial Day*
Flag Day • *Father's Day* • *Independence Day* • *Labor Day*
Columbus Day • *Veteran's Day* • *Thanksgiving* • *Christmas*

To order, visit your bookstore or call The Summit Group: 1-800-875-3346